Writers Uncovered

JAN MARK

Vic Parker

Heinemann
LIBRARY

www.heinemann.co.uk/library
Visit our website to find out more information about Heinemann Library books.

To order:

☎ Phone 44 (0) 1865 888066

🖹 Send a fax to 44 (0) 1865 314091

💻 Visit the Heinemann bookshop at www.heinemann.co.uk/library to browse our catalogue and order online.

First published in Great Britain by Heinemann Library, Halley Court, Jordan Hill, Oxford OX2 8EJ, part of Harcourt Education.

Heinemann is a registered trademark of Harcourt Education Ltd.

Editorial: Charlotte Guillain and Dave Harris
Design: Richard Parker and Q2A Solutions
Picture research: Hannah Taylor and Bea Ray
Production: Duncan Gilbert

Originated by Chroma Graphics (O) Pte Ltd.
Printed and bound in China by
  South China Printing Company

10 digit ISBN: 0 431 90631 9
13 digit ISBN: 978 0 431 90631 7

10 09 08 07 06
10 9 8 7 6 5 4 3 2 1

British Library Cataloguing in Publication Data
Parker, Vic
  Jan Mark. – (Writers uncovered)
  823.9'14
A full catalogue record for this book is available from the British Library.

Acknowledgements
The publishers would like to thank the following for permission to reproduce photographs:
Alamy Images p. **15** (Dave Gowans); Bernadette Watts p. **13**; Carnival p. **20**; Corbis p. **11** (Robbie Jack); Getty Images p. **22** (Hulton Archive); Harcourt Education Ltd pp. **4**, **17**, **18**, **21**, **24**, **25**, **26** (Tudor Photography); HarperCollins p. **9**; Jan Mark pp. **6**, **7**, **8**, **10**, **12**, **14**, **36**, **42**; Oxford University Press p. **31**; Puffin pp. **29**, **33**; Random House pp. **39a**, **39b**; Rex Features p. **37**; Scholastic p. **35**; Vinmag p. **23**.

p. **27**: *Riding Tycho* manuscript reproduced by permission of David Higham Associates on behalf of Jan Mark.

Every effort has been made to contact copyright holders of any material reproduced in this book. Any omissions will be rectified in subsequent printings if notice is given to the publishers.

The paper used to print this book comes from sustainable resources.

CONTENTS

An author with class 4

Jan grows up 6

Off into the world 12

Jan the author 16

Jan's work 26

Thunder and Lightnings 28

The Ennead 30

Handles 32

The Eclipse of the Century 34

Prizes, points of view, and praise 36

Remembering Jan Mark 42

Timeline 44

Further resources 46

Glossary 47

Index 48

Words appearing in the text in bold, **like this**,
are explained in the glossary.

AN AUTHOR WITH CLASS

Jan Mark was one of the book world's hidden treasures. Her stories, **anthologies**, and plays are among readers' favourites the world over. She was also a trusted book reviewer and wrote regularly for newspapers and magazines. Librarians, booksellers, and publishers are in awe of her astonishing ideas and writing skills, and awarded her many top prizes. However, many of Jan's fans know almost nothing about her life. They have no idea what she looked like, where she lived, or anything about her background. If you are one of these intrigued readers, just read on…

Here is Jan outside the house where she wrote many of her stories.

Why was Jan such an outstanding writer?

There are not many authors who can write popular books for every age group, but Jan could. She mastered the art of writing picture books, short stories, and novels which appeal to both young people and adults. Jan did not see herself as a children's author, just as an author. She once said: "I do not write specifically for children, any more than I write for adults. I tend rather to write about children."

Jan's award-winning novels contain astonishingly different and original ideas, written in familiar but fresh and often funny **prose**. They are thought-provoking, challenging reads. If you have come across any, you will know that diving into a Jan Mark story can be a brain-sizzling experience.

FIND OUT MORE...

Here are some of Jan's favourite things:

Favourite food...	Pickled herrings.
Favourite music...	*Klezmer* – which is a type of Jewish "knees-up" music.
Favourite film...	*Ulysses' Gaze*, which is a very long film that few people have heard of or seen.
Favourite animal...	Rats – Jan greatly admired these intelligent creatures and wrote a book about them for young children.
Favourite colour...	Yellow.
Favourite saying...	"Anything that can happen, can happen to you!"

JAN GROWS UP

Jan was born on 22 June 1943. This was during the terrible time of World War II. Jan's parents, Colin and Marjorie Brisland, came from London, but Jan was born in a hospital in Welwyn, Hertfordshire because London was bombed so often. Colin was a **journalist**. Marjorie was a **seamstress** who specialised in big, heavy jobs such as **upholstery** and making theatre curtains.

This is young Jan at ten months old.

FIND OUT MORE...

In World War II (1939–1945), many nations, including Britain, France, Russia, and the United States, fought against Germany, Japan, and Italy. Over 45 million people were killed and millions more were injured. Cities all over Europe were reduced to rubble, and there were shortages of homes, food and supplies which lasted for many years after the war ended.

Education at home

Jan's mother taught Jan to read at a very early age. She knew all the letters of the alphabet by the age of two-and-a-half years old, and had joined the library by the age of five! After Jan's mother realised that Jan needed glasses, Jan found reading even easier. As soon as Jan could read, she also enjoyed trying to write. She covered pages and pages with scribble-written stories.

Growing up with grandma

Jan's parents soon had a son, called Martyn. The family lived for a few years in Jan's grandmother's home, in North Finchley in London. The area was crammed with **semi-detached** houses from the 1930s, just like theirs. Jan liked living with her grandma very much.

Jan had many happy memories of the time she lived at her grandmother's home in London.

This is Hollington school at the time Jan went there in the early 1950s.

A move to the country

When Jan was six years old, the family went to live in Kent. They stayed in Chatham for about six months before going to Ashford. Jan missed her grandma – and her grandma's cats. She could not have a cat of her own because her family moved a lot, from one rented house to another.

Starting school

Jan's mother taught her at home for a while. Then, when Jan was seven-and-a-half years old, she started at Hollington School. Jan enjoyed school – especially English lessons, when she could read and write stories to her heart's content. Jan wrote endlessly at home too, bashing out tales on her dad's typewriter.

Family changes

Jan's father often worked away from home and, when Jan was nine, he finally left the family. It was a tough time, but soon Jan, her brother and her mother settled into a comfortable **council house**.

Living at the library

Jan adored books and spent hours at the library, hunting out good reads. Jan had unusual taste in stories. Some of her favourites are *King Purple's Jester* by D.H. Chapman, *Caterpillar Hall* by Anne Barrett, and *Larking at Christmas* by Judith Masefield.

INSIDE INFORMATION

The illustrations in *Larking at Christmas* were done by an artist called Shirley Hughes. Jan loved the drawings and she used to look out for books by Shirley. They sparked off Jan's life-long interest in art, and her love of illustrations in books.

Shirley Hughes's illustrations are simple and eye-catching.

Jan loved to act in school plays. Here she is in Shakespeare's *Much Ado About Nothing*.

An inspiring teacher

At the age of eleven, Jan passed the exam to go to Ashford Grammar School. Her favourite teacher there was the head of English and Music, Mary Mitchell. Miss Mitchell was passionate about Shakespeare and the theatre, and used to organise drama competitions and school plays. Jan enjoyed acting, but also became very interested in scenery, lighting, costumes, and directing. Jan also loved music. She sang in Miss Mitchell's singing groups, and often performed in concerts.

Could do better

Jan was excellent at Art as well as English and Music, but she just scraped by in other subjects. Jan was particularly dreadful at science; she found it impossible to understand how the theories and concepts fitted into real life. Later on, she also thought that history was taught in a boring way.

Writer in training

Jan never did her homework properly because she was far too busy reading and writing stories! At the age of fifteen she entered a short story in a competition organised by the *Daily Mirror* newspaper. She was one of ten runners up. Jan was also working on a long novel, creating an opera with a friend, inventing poems, and writing plays. Jan dreamed of being a published writer one day, although she never imagined she would be able to earn a living from it.

INSIDE INFORMATION

As a teenager, Jan loved the plays of George Bernard Shaw, such as *Pygmalion*. She read them as if they were novels, and admired the realistic **dialogue**. Dialogue-writing later became one of Jan's own special skills.

Pygmalion is about a language professor who tries to turn a poor Cockney flower girl into an upper-class woman.

Jan stayed on at school until she was eighteen. Most pupils who took A-Level exams, like her, went to university or training college rather than straight into a job. Jan would have loved to go on to music college or even perhaps drama school, but she knew that these places were far too expensive. Instead, Jan decided to go to art school, like her friend from the year above, Bernadette Watts. Bernadette later became a well-known **illustrator**.

Jan the art student

Jan went to Canterbury College of Art to study for four years for a National **Diploma** in Design. She loved the creativity of her course, and also found it exciting to live away from home for the first time, sharing a flat with friends.

Jan planned to be a teacher after she finished at college. However, she was determined to continue writing and have a book published one day. A couple of times Jan tried sending a short story to a magazine, but disappointingly, the stories were never printed.

Jan discovered at art college that she had a special talent for sculpture.

BROTHERS GRIMM

JORINDA and JORINDEL

Retold and illustrated by
BERNADETTE WATTS

Bernadette Watts is now an illustrator of picture books.

Jan starts work

In 1965, Jan went to be an Art and English teacher at Southfields School, Gravesend. With all the lesson preparation and marking, teaching was hard work. It did not leave Jan much time or energy to write. However, she did write two plays which the school put on.

FIND OUT MORE...

Jan particularly enjoyed teaching the work of William Shakespeare. *Hamlet* led her later to write *Heathrow Nights*, and *A Midsummer Night's Dream* inspired *Stratford Boys*.

New beginnings

While Jan was teaching at Southfields School, one of her colleagues introduced her to a friend called Neil Mark. Neil worked as a computer operator, which Jan found fascinating as computers were very new in those days. Jan and Neil soon fell in love and got married. They were delighted when a daughter, Isobel, was born in 1969.

Two years later, Neil was offered an interesting new job. Unfortunately, the job was in a different part of the country, Norfolk. Jan had to leave Southfields School so she and Neil could move to Norfolk, and she decided to have a break from teaching for a while. The family settled in a small village near the sea called Ingham, and in 1974 Jan gave birth to a baby son, who they named Alex.

The young family at the seaside near their home in Norfolk.

Jan's first novel was about BAC Lightning jet fighter planes like this one.

A book at last!

Jan thought that when her children were at school, she would return to teaching. Meanwhile, she enjoyed looking after her young family and writing when she could. One day, Jan noticed a competition in *The Guardian* newspaper. It was for a children's novel set in the 20th century, by an author who had not had a book published before. Jan immediately thought of something to write about: her home was near an RAF airbase and every day the BAC Lightning jet fighter planes roared overhead. To Jan's amazement and delight, her story, *Thunder and Lightnings*, won the competition and was published as a book.

FIND OUT MORE...

The runner-up in the novel competition that Jan won was Anne Fine who, like Jan, has since become a best-selling author. Anne's novel was published too. It was called *The Summer House Loon*.

Jan had been writing on her own all her life, but suddenly everyone wanted to know about her and her work. A top **literary agent** offered to work for Jan, arranging for her stories to be published. Jan set about writing more books with renewed energy and enthusiasm.

A variety of styles and ideas

Jan aimed her second novel at the same age group as her first: nine- to twelve-year-olds. It was called *Under the Autumn Garden* and was published in 1977. This was the same year that *Thunder and Lightnings* was awarded a top prize called the Carnegie Medal, which was an amazing achievement for a first novel. Then Jan tried something completely different: three books for teenagers, beginning with *The Ennead* (1978), then *Divide and Rule* (1980) and *Aquarius* (1982).

The long and short of writing

At the same time Jan turned her hand to short stories as well. A collection called *Nothing to be Afraid Of* was published in 1980 and another, *Hairs in the Palm of the Hand*, was published in 1981. Jan had loved short stories ever since she was little. Magazines for children and adults regularly published short stories until the 1960s, with eye-catching line drawings and interesting photographs. Jan's all-time favourite authors included short-story writers such as Gerald Kersh, Rudyard Kipling, Guy Maupassant and Saki (H.H. Munro).

HAVE A GO

HAVE A GO

Try writing your own short story. When you have finished, think about how you could retell it in a longer way, to make it into a novel with chapters. You could extend scenes from your short story, or add new scenes. Which way do you think would work best for your story? Would you prefer to write short stories or novels?

Jan loved to read the short stories in magazines like these.

Jan felt that writing novels and writing short stories are two totally different skills. She enjoyed doing both precisely because they are very separate crafts. A short story has its own unique pace – it can focus on a single event in a very intense way, or it can race through an entire fast-moving, **suspenseful** tale. Jan felt that what a short story does best is to catch people at the moment something life-changing happens.

Back to college

Around this time, Jan's publisher told her about a job advertisement. It was for the position of Writer in Residence at a college called Oxford Polytechnic. Jan was interested because the post was in the education department. Jan thought she could put both her teaching experience and her writing talents to good use. She was thrilled when she got the job – even though it meant staying in a flat on **campus** during the week and travelling back to her family in Norfolk for the weekends.

Oxford Polytechnic is now called Oxford Brookes University.

Another award-winning novel

Many of Jan's colleagues suspected that Jan was there to do secret research for a novel about college life. They were totally wrong! But Jan did write a novel during her first term. It was called *Handles* – and it also won the Carnegie Medal.

Teaching teachers

The polytechnic left it up to Jan to decide how she should spend her time. She decided that she wanted to work with students who were training to be teachers. Jan watched the student teachers gaining experience in classrooms and realised that they were under a lot of pressure. They had heavy timetables and unreasonable expectations placed upon them. Jan thought that if she could make teaching more fun for teachers, then she could make learning more fun for the pupils.

Jan realised that many of the student teachers were trying to teach their pupils to be good readers and writers, when they themselves had not read a children's book or written anything since they were young. Jan helped the student teachers explore inspiring books in the children's section of the library, and introduced creative writing as part of their course. Together, they came up with all sorts of exciting ideas for classwork.

HAVE A GO

One tip Jan gave to anyone who wants to be a good writer is to read, read, and then read some more! Do not just stick to the authors you know well or your favourite type of books – read anything and everything you can lay your hands on. Start off by stealing ideas from other writers, then play around with them and change them to make them your own. One day you will find that you do not need to steal ideas any more...

Books, books, and more books

Jan's position as Writer in Residence at Oxford Polytechnic ended in 1984. Unfortunately, she and her husband had grown apart. The couple decided to split, and Jan moved to a home in Oxford.

Jan continued to write all sorts of books, for readers of all ages. She wrote picture books for toddlers and very young children, such as *Carrot Tops and Cotton Tails*, illustrated by Tony Ross. Jan adapted novels for broadcasting on the radio and turned them into plays for television programmes such as *Middle English*. She wrote children's **non-fiction**, such as a book on aeroplanes and another on museums. She also wrote one novel for adults, called *Zeno Was Here*, and many others for young people.

Carrot Tops and Cottontails is Jan's best-selling picture book.

HAVE A GO

How would you turn your favourite story into a play for television? Here are some things to think about:

- You could just use dialogue and action to tell your audience what your characters are thinking and feeling, or you could have a character who sometimes speaks directly to the audience, or perhaps a **narrator**.
- You could order events by starting at the beginning and working **chronologically** through to the end, or you could use "flashback" scenes of the past and "dream" scenes of the future.
- Break your action up into scenes that take place in different settings.
- Try to make your characters' speech realistic.
- Include in your script brief instructions to the actors about how to move on stage or speak their lines.
- Suggest some special effects, stunts, or music!

Jan lived in the historic city of Oxford.

Ideas from real life

Jan never based a character in her novels on herself or her children, but sometimes she used her experiences as starting points for stories. For instance, when Jan was a student, she got a summer job at a pub outside Ashford. Twenty one years later, she wrote a novel about the place called *At the Sign of the Dog and Rocket* (1985).

Jan saved up another experience for around 40 years before writing about it. *Something in the Air* (2003) is based on how she used to hear **Morse code** inside her head when she was a teenager. No one believed her at the time, but when Jan was writing the book she finally discovered the explanation: some people can pick up radio signals through their wire-framed glasses or the fillings in their teeth!

From the late 19th century, Morse code was used for sending messages quickly over long distances. Operators like these had to work out what the messages said.

INSIDE INFORMATION

Some of Jan's best ideas were accidental discoveries. When Jan was writing *Riding Tycho*, she noticed after about 60 pages that she had not mentioned birds. She decided that the world she was creating should have no concept of flight – and the plot took a direction she would never have planned.

Inspiration from interests

Strangely enough, Jan became obsessed with the subjects she enjoyed the least at school: history and science. Her ideas for novels could be sparked off by ancient objects in museums or by thought-provoking articles and photographs in magazines such as the *Fortean Times*. Jan combined her passion for the past and her fascination with the future in *Useful Idiots* (2004). In this book, she imagined the world in 2255, when history has been forgotten and the study of **archaeology** has been outlawed.

Fortean Times magazine contains weird and wonderful articles that fired Jan's imagination.

Being Jan Mark

Jan never ran short of ideas for stories and wrote about two books a year. Each story took a lot of time to research, and Jan often had to go out and about to find out information. At the same time as Jan wrote a new story, she usually had to make revisions to her previous story too, and also check **proofs** of the story she wrote before that. It was lucky that Jan did not get stressed under pressure. In fact, she liked working to deadlines. Jan also sometimes taught creative writing to adults, such as on courses for people who want to be authors. She was also in great demand for school and library visits.

Jan liked spending time in her garden to relax.

Jan hated going on holiday because she disliked feeling like a tourist. When she travelled abroad to work, she much preferred to stay with the people who lived there, to be shown around as their guest.

Jan lived in a small **Victorian terraced** house in east Oxford. She moved there after her marriage ended, and lived there until she died on 16 January 2006 at the age of 62.

Jan at work on her trusty old typewriter.

FIND OUT MORE...

When Jan was not writing, she loved watching films. She thought that you can learn as much about storytelling from a good film as you can from a good book. Jan built up a huge video collection by recording her favourite films off the television.

Jan liked writing stories at her kitchen table.

Jan used a room in her house as an office, but she did not write her stories there. This was partly because the office was full of paperwork, and partly because she preferred to write in her kitchen. The kitchen was sunny and warm because it had a big, south-facing window.

Jan did not plan her stories in detail before she started writing them. As soon as she had enough of an idea, she began to write and let the story develop as she wrote it. When Jan was less experienced, she sometimes got **writer's block** and panicked. She found that leaving her writing for a while and coming back to it later always helped her see things from a different point of view and get going again.

Work in progress

Jan always wrote the first **draft** of a **manuscript** using a pen and an A4 notepad. She wrote further drafts on a typewriter, not a computer. This was because Jan preferred the look of typed pages to computer print-outs, and also out of habit. Jan used an electric typewriter for eighteen years until it finally gave up. She then replaced it with one exactly the same! Jan usually wrote about three drafts of a manuscript. She had good **editors** and was happy to make revisions to her text.

73

She had never been this far, this high. The of fields lay below them, then the ridge over which they had walked and now the town was in sight again. She could not believe how sma it was, the rooftops clustering along the sides of the Blackwater, to the harbour and the rocks. The mole was no more than an eyebrow in the sea. The beach was out of sight the wind about them.

As they came out on to the cliff top the wind about them.

Strangely it was less violent up here, but much colder. She stood looking all round. Back the way they had come lay the town. Had s not known what it was she would have thought the rooftops were haph slabs of rock where the stream had cut its way down to the harbour. looked like a cascade of stones, and for the first time she saw why it was there, in the little bay scooped out by Tycho, the one place where you could get on and off the island.

Ahead the land continued to rise and fall, but each time rising higher than before, then gathering itself into a green up to the peak, still white-capped with snow as the were a frozen wave.

On the lower slopes were little grey-white dots of snow. But – '

'Look! They're moving.'

'They're sheep,' Ianto Morgan said. 'Dear chil knitting, have you never seen a sheep?'

'Knitting?' Oh, the wool. I've seen pictures.

'Well, there's the real thing. So they let the hills here, and they'll lamb in spring, the old wa ever come up here

'I don't know. The shepherds bring the wool. It isn't on the sheep, 'where do they live?'

'I don't know.'

'There used to be an observatory out there, on plateau. A place to study the stars,' he said, Telescopes.

'To look through?'

'Some went, but there was a radio telescope, too.

This is a page from the second draft of *Riding Tycho*, showing all of Jan's scribbles and notes.

INSIDE INFORMATION

Jan liked to give her stories open endings. Her fans often begged her to tell them what happens. However, Jan did not think about her novels beyond what she wrote. She liked readers to finish off her stories for themselves.

THUNDER AND LIGHTNINGS

Main characters

Andrew Mitchell .... a twelve-year-old city boy whose interests are motor-racing and keeping guinea pigs

Andrew's mother ... who used to be a librarian, before she had children and stopped working

Andrew's father ..... who works with computers and was brought up in the countryside

Edward .... Andrew's baby brother

Victor Skelton .... an eccentric, interesting boy who is in Andrew's class at school

Victor's parents ..... an old-fashioned, stern, unaffectionate couple

The plot

When Andrew's family move to a small village on the Norfolk coast, he makes friends with one of his new neighbours, Victor. Victor is a wealth of fascinating information on many subjects that interest him – including the British military aircraft which fly overhead every day from a nearby RAF base. Victor's passion sparks enthusiasm in Andrew too, and together the boys spend the summer tracking the aeroplanes. Victor is especially crazy about the BAC Lightning jet fighters – but how will he take it when he finds out that his precious planes are to be scrapped in favour of new Jaguars?

INSIDE INFORMATION

Several times while Jan was writing *Thunder and Lightnings* she felt it was no good and nearly gave up. In the end, it proved to be her breakthrough into being a published writer. Looking back, Jan felt that she was in the right place, at the right time, doing the right thing. Her subject matter was passing overhead every day, she did not have a full-time job so she had time to write, and she kept going even when she had doubts.

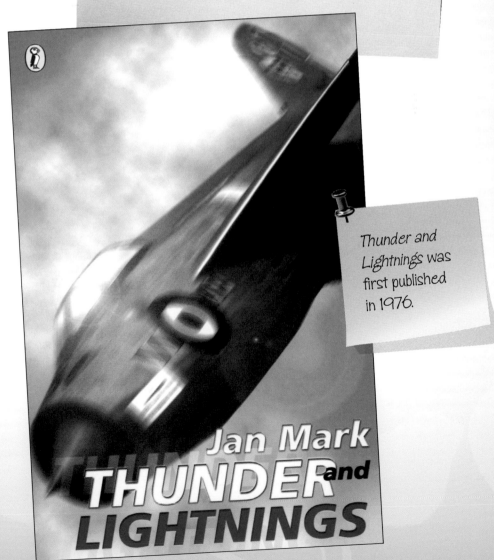

Jan Mark
THUNDER and
LIGHTNINGS

Thunder and Lightnings was first published in 1976.

THE ENNEAD

Main characters

Isaac .... a fifteen-year-old orphan boy,
living by his wits
Theodore Swenson ... head of the Intergalactic Freight
Company, whose father adopted
Isaac when he was five
Loukides .... Sergeant of Colonial Police
Cameron .... the wealthy town magistrate
Gregor .... Cameron's influential steward
Moshe .... Cameron's gardener
Eleanor Ashe .... a sculptor, from another planet

The plot

Earth has long been dying, causing a flood of refugees to other planets in the system of nine known as the Ennead. The authorities on the planet Erato are determined to control **immigration** of the **refugees** rigidly, and to keep law and order by enforcing a strict system of rules and regulations.

Isaac was seen as an outsider until his fifteenth birthday, when he managed to wangle an official position for himself as steward of Theodore's household. Now he must do whatever it takes to keep his post; but Isaac is fed up of bowing and scraping to elders and bribing officials. He wants to have power over someone else.

An opportunity arises to bring a female sculptor from Euterpe, which would put her forever into Isaac's debt. Isaac seizes the chance but Eleanor Ashe is nothing like the beautiful, timid girl he expects. Her stubborn independence and fighting spirit attract an unexpected friend in Moshe, and awaken long-forgotten ideas from Earth, which can only mean big trouble.

INSIDE INFORMATION

When Jan was a student at Canterbury College of Art, her course gave her the opportunity to explore many different art forms. Jan discovered that she had a talent for sculpture and carving, just like Eleanor Ashe.

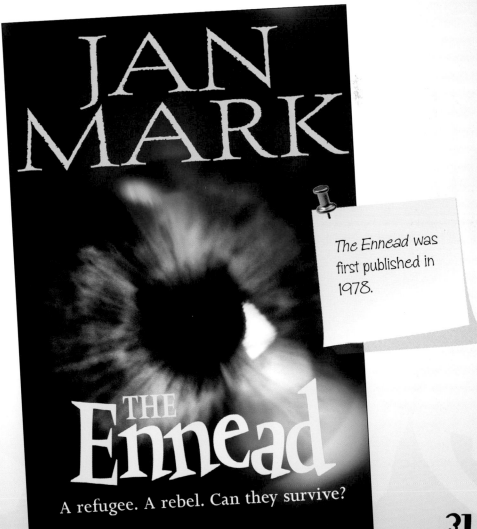

JAN MARK

THE Ennead

A refugee. A rebel. Can they survive?

The Ennead was first published in 1978.

HANDLES

Main characters

Erica Timperley ...... a tomboy with a passion
for motorbikes

Joan .... Erica's nagging auntie

Peter .... Erica's stiff uncle

Robert .... Erica's lazy, irritating cousin

Elsie .... whose real name is Lynden –
the owner of a motorbike workshop

Bunny .... whose real name is Bernard –
a mechanic at the workshop

Ted Hales .... an old pig farmer

The plot

Erica Timperley is a city girl, all set to spend her school holidays hanging out with a crowd of bikers in the multi-storey car park. Then her mum springs a surprise – Erica is being packed off to the countryside to stay with relatives. Erica faces weeks of digging vegetables from the family garden to sell at their roadside stall.

However, Erica discovers a tiny, tucked away industrial estate and starts spending her days at a motorbike workshop. The characters Erica encounters there do not use their regular names; they have "handles", such as Kermit and the Gremlin. But will Erica be admitted properly into this secret, special world by being given a handle of her own?

WINNER OF THE CARNEGIE MEDAL

Handles

JAN MARK

Handles was published in 1983.

INSIDE INFORMATION

Jan found the inspiration for *Handles* through people she met when she lived in Ingham. Her husband had a friend who owned a small motorbike repair shop nearby, and he would sometimes go there to help out. One day, he came home bursting with excitement about a very rare bike that had arrived at the shop for renovation: an Indian. The seeds of a story had been sown in Jan's mind…

THE ECLIPSE OF THE CENTURY

Main characters

Keith Chapman .... a twenty-year-old student
Lieutenants Kijé
 and Fitzgibbon .... two soldiers based at Control Point E
Szusko......................... a coalman, who has a pet bear
Ernestine Fahrenheit .. the widow of a museum curator
Lady Maisie Hooke ..... the senile old widow of a spy-diplomat
Zayu .... a young woman from a nomadic
 people called the Sturyat

The plot

When Keith is in a terrible car crash on the motorway, he seems to float out of his body and through a long tunnel to a strange place. A woman tells him he is in Kantoom and that they will meet again "under a black sun at the end of a thousand years". Keith thinks that this "near death experience" is probably all in his mind – but then he discovers that Qantoum is a real town in a forsaken part of Asia.

Keith feels that he'll never rest unless he finds out if his dream means anything, so he travels there. He finds himself caught up in a dispute between a ragtag community who live in Qantoum and a local tribe called the Sturyat. But does his arrival really fulfil an ancient Sturyat prophecy? Are their beliefs linked to the arrival of the year 2000? And has Keith accidentally started a rush of other Westerners into the area, all with their own expectations?

THE ECLIPSE OF THE CENTURY

"Read it and be amazed."
PHILIP PULLMAN

The Eclipse of the Century is enjoyed as much by adults as by young people.

Jan Mark

INSIDE INFORMATION

Jan started writing *The Eclipse of the Century* in 1996, when she was wondering about what people believed might happen to the world at the turn of the new millennium. The story opens in April 1999, which is the date the book was published.

There are not many writers who have won the Carnegie Medal twice, like Jan did. The Carnegie Medal is awarded by librarians and is one of the most prestigious honours in children's book publishing. Jan's work has also been showered with other awards too. Here are some of them:

- *Aquarius* won The Rank/Observer Prize for Teenage Fiction
- Both *Feet and Other Stories* and *Zeno Was Here* won The Angel Award for Fiction
- The short story collection *Nothing to be Afraid Of* was highly commended for the Carnegie Medal
- *The Eclipse of the Century* was **shortlisted** for the Guardian Children's Fiction Award
- *Thunder and Lightnings* was named a Notable Children's Book by the American Library Association.

Here is Jan (on the front row, at the bottom left of the photo) when her first novel, *Thunder and Lightnings*, won *The Guardian* newspaper competition in 1975.

Distinguished honours

The book world holds Jan in high regard. In 1984, she was chosen as the British entrant for the international Hans Christian Andersen Medal. Publishers often asked Jan to put together anthologies of stories and poetry, such as *The Puffin Book of Song and Dance*, and *The Oxford Book of Children's Stories*. Jan was a big poetry fan – she sometimes wrote poems herself and had one small book of them published.

FIND OUT MORE...

In 1987, a film director called Michael Winterbottom turned Jan's novel *Trouble Half-Way* into a three part serial for schools' television. The story tells of a journey a lorry driver takes with his stepdaughter. Michael Winterbottom made a fourth part, where Jan did the journey in the story for real, in her brother's furniture van!

The director Michael Winterbottom has since become famous for his work on many other films.

A respected reviewer

Newspapers and magazines employ people called critics to write their opinions of stories as book reviews. As well as being a top author, Jan was a leading critic of young people's books. Her reviews regularly appeared in *The Guardian*, the *Times Educational Supplement*, and *Carousel*. Jan's opinions were in great demand.

Jan used to be sent so many books in the hope that she would review them that she did not know what to do with them all! They overflowed from cupboards and ended up in heaps on the floor, stacks on the stairs, and mounds under the bed. Jan read endless stories for reviewing so, for fun, she preferred reading non-fiction, such as books about physics and military history.

Recommended reads

A critic's job is a responsible one, because their reviews help readers to decide whether to spend their time and money on a story or not. Jan felt that too many books are praised and acclaimed as outstanding when they do not deserve to be. Jan herself was very careful with her praise. She aimed to search out books which might not be obvious best-sellers, but which were treasures that no one else seemed to have noticed.

INSIDE INFORMATION

One "little gem" Jan discovered in her work as a critic is *Keeper* by Mal Peet. The entire novel takes place in a newspaper office in South America, where a top football writer is interviewing El Gato, the world's best goalkeeper. On the table between them stands the World Cup. El Gato tells a strange tale about being trained by a ghost in the middle of the rainforest. Want to know more? You will have to read it for yourself!

Forgotten favourites

Jan said that three of her own books were misread by various critics, who gave them reviews that she found very puzzling. She feels that as a result the stories were ignored by people who would enjoy them, and are now somewhat "forgotten". This is one reason why Jan was so careful when she wrote reviews of other authors' work.

The first of these books was one of Jan's favourites out of all her work: *Enough is Too Much Already*. It is made up of seven short stories about the same three people, and is told entirely in dialogue. The second book is *The Hillingdon Fox*, which was inspired by two wars: the Gulf War of the early 1990s and the Falklands War of the early 1980s. The third book is *They Do Things Differently There*, which the top writer Adèle Geras has said "should be a cult classic".

Enough is Too Much Already was published in 1988.

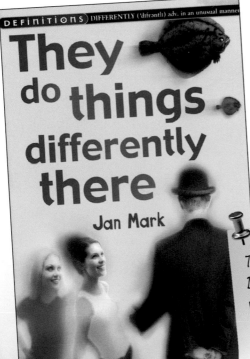

They Do Things Differently There was published in 1994.

Views in the news

Here's an example of a review for *Heathrow Nights*, with some notes on how the critic has put it together. Would it encourage you to read the book?

What do you think of Shakespeare? Fifteen-year-old Russell wasn't a fan until he came across *Hamlet*. He and the Prince of Denmark seem to have a lot in common – their fathers have both died, their mothers have remarried too hastily, and they each hate their new stepdad. Russell can't stop thinking about the play – so why did he join in with his two best mates to wreck a performance at the Theatre Royal by heckling the actors? Besides being thrown out of the theatre, the three troublemakers face exclusion from school and are banned from going on their half-term trip.

They can't bring themselves to tell their families, so instead, they bunk off down to London. With nowhere to stay and very little money, Russell decides that Heathrow Airport is the perfect place to hide up for the week. But he has nothing to do except think about his life, his emotions, his memories – and *Hamlet*…

Heathrow Nights is a challenging yet fun novel for older children. Its familiar language, realistic dialogue, and easy style make it an enjoyable, effortless read. *Heathrow Nights* has all the richness of real life – from humour to sadness, from gritty everyday problems to magical possibilities.

Jan Mark is an award-winning author of many thought-provoking books for young people, including *Thunder and Lightnings* and *Handles*. *Heathrow Nights* should be on the reading wish list of anyone aged twelve or over.

a little about the story, without giving too much away

a summary of what kind of book it is and who the book is aimed at

the critic's opinion on whether it is a good or bad read, with clear reasons

some background on the author and comparison with other types of work

a recommendation of who the critic thinks will like the book

HAVE A GO

Why not try writing your own review of a Jan Mark book? You could then give your review to a friend who does not know the story and see if they go on to read it. Ask them to write a review back, recommending one of their own favourite reads to you. You might discover a great new book or author...

Pieces of praise

Here are some of the rave reviews that critics have given Jan's work:

"...she's one of those writers who (like Shakespeare) can turn her hand to anything. Domestic drama, science fiction, ghost stories, millennial angst, picture books, teenage chit-chat: you name it..."

author Adèle Geras

"This book is extraordinary. Long, intense, dreamlike, it's more like a piece of music than a novel ... read it, and be amazed."

award-winning author Philip Pullman on
The Eclipse of the Century

"The best books leave the reader wondering how the author came up with the idea, and this is one of them."

The University of Strathclyde Library service on
The Eclipse of the Century

Stories were Jan's lifelong passion. As she herself once said: "Almost everything I do is connected with books and writing". Jan's main ambition was to be a writer, and she accomplished just that. Jan was content with her life and happy with everything she achieved.

Inspiring her readers

Jan particularly enjoyed talking about her books during school visits. She encouraged children to take reading and writing seriously, and was full of praise for those that did.

She was delighted to have struck up a relationship with a group of schools in Flanders, Belgium. Jan travelled there every year to talk about books and explore writing ideas with the teenage pupils.

Jan works with a student in Belgium.

Writing in focus

Jan's books have lots of fans worldwide. Here is what some of them think about *The Eclipse of the Century*:

"This would be perfect to be made into a movie. The characters are so real and vivid, especially Lieutenant Kije. You want to reach in and help everyone find the answers..."
Lauren, age 14, from Hampshire

"I've re-read this book more than any other. The plot twists and turns like a snake, the characters seem to leap from the pages, I absolutely love it!"
Simon, age 17, from London

VOYAGER

Jan died on 16 January 2006, but her fans will remember her as a hugely talented writer who produced over 50 amazing books. *Voyager*, the sequel to *Riding Tycho*, was released shortly before Jan died, on 6 January 2006.

Voyager continues the story of a girl named Demetria, who is plucked from the ocean by the crew of the *Laurentia Bay*. Having risked everything to escape her life on High Island, she desperately hopes that she is finally free. But the world beyond the island is an even more terrifying place where castaways like Demetria are accused of being enemy spies. Far from being over, it seeems her struggle for freedom has only just begun.

Voyager is an essential read for fans of Jan's work.

TIMELINE

1943   Jan Brisland is born on June 22.

1950   Jan starts at Hollington School.

1954   Jan passes the entry exam for Ashford Grammar School.

1958   Jan is one of ten runners-up in a short story competition organized by the *Daily Mirror* newspaper.

1961   Jan goes to Canterbury College of Art to study for a National Diploma in Design.

1965   Jan starts work as an Art and English teacher at Southfields School, Gravesend.

1969   Jan marries Neil Mark.
Jan and Neil's daughter, Isobel, is born.

1971   Jan, Neil, and Isobel move to Ingham in Norfolk.

1974   Jan and Neil's son, Alex, is born.

1975   Jan wins a competition run by *The Guardian* newspaper with her story, *Thunder and Lightnings*.

1976   *Thunder and Lightnings* is published.

1977   *Thunder and Lightnings* wins the Carnegie Medal. It is also named a Notable Children's Book by the American Library Association.
Under the Autumn Garden is published.

1978   *The Ennead* is published.

1979   *Divide and Rule* is published.

1980   *Nothing to Be Afraid Of* is published, and is highly commended for the Carnegie Medal.
The Short Voyage of the Albert Ross is published.

1981   *Hairs in the Palm of the Hand* and *The Long Distance Poet* are published.

1982   Jan becomes Writer in Residence at Oxford Polytechnic.
Aquarius is published, and wins The Rank/Observer Prize for Teenage Fiction.
The Dead Letter Box is published.

1983   *Handles* is published and wins the Carnegie Medal.
Feet and Other Stories wins the Angel Award for Fiction.

1984   Jan splits from Neil and settles permanently in Oxford.
Jan is chosen as the British entrant for the international Hans Christian Andersen Medal.
Childermas is published.

1985 *Trouble Half-Way* and *At the Sign of the Dog and Rocket* are published.

1987 The film director Michael Winterbottom turns *Trouble Half-Way* into a three part serial for schools' television.
Zeno Was Here is published and wins the Angel Award for Fiction

1988 *Enough is Too Much Already*, *Presents From Gran*, and *The Twig Thing* are published.

1990 *Finders, Losers* and *A Can of Worms and Other Stories* are published.
A play called *Time and the Hour* is published.

1991 *The Hillingdon Fox*, and *In Black & White And Other Stories* are published.

1992 *The Snow Maze*, *Great Frog and Mighty Moose*, and *The Puffin Book of Song and Dance* are published.

1993 *Carrot Tops and Cottontails*, *All the Kings and Queens*, *This Bowl of Earth*, *Fun with Mrs Thumb*, and *The Oxford Book of Children's Stories* are published.

1994 *They Do Things Differently There*, *Taking the Cat's Way Home*, *A Worm's Eye View*, *Harriet's Turn*, and *Haddock* are published.

1995 *A Fine Summer Knight* and *The Tale of Tobias* are published.

1996 *Under the Red Elephant* is published.

1997 *The Sighting*, *The Coconut Quins*, *My Frog and I*, and *God's Story* are published.

1998 *Worry-Guts* is published.

1999 *The Eclipse of the Century* is published and is shortlisted for the Guardian Children's Fiction Award.
Lady-Long-Legs and *The Midas Touch* are published.

2000 *Heathrow Nights* and *The Lady With Iron Bones* are published.

2001 *Mr Dickens Hits Town*, *Rats* and *Shipwrecks* are published.

2002 *Long Lost* is published.

2003 *Something in the Air*, *A Jetblack Sunrise*, *Eyes Wide Open*, *Stratford Boys*, and *Aeroplanes* are published.

2004 *Useful Idiots* is published.

2005 *Riding Tycho*, *The Electric Telepath* and *Turbulence* are published.

2006 Jan dies on January 16 at the age of 62.

FURTHER RESOURCES

More books to read

Children's Books and Their Creators, Anita Silvey, (Houghton Mifflin, 1996)

The Oxford Book of Children's Stories, Jan Mark (editor) (Oxford, 2001)

Audiobooks

Versions of many of Jan's stories are also available as audiobooks on CD and cassette, including:

Heathrow Nights (Chivers Children's Audio Books, 2002)

Stratford Boys (Hodder Children's Audio Books, 2004)

Thunder and Lightnings (Chivers Children's Audio Books, 1991)

Websites

A site all about books for young people:
www.booktrusted.co.uk

A site recommending books for young people, with many book reviews:
www.readingmatters.co.uk

A site devoted to short stories:
www.short-stories.co.uk

GLOSSARY

anthology   collection of work by different people

archaeology   science of studying historical remains and ruins

campus   buildings and grounds of a college or university

chronological   in time order, from start to finish

council house   house owned by the council

dialogue   speech, conversation

diploma   type of educational certificate

draft   version of a piece of work before it is finished

editor   person in a publishing company who oversees the words of a book

illustrator   person who draws pictures to go with writing

immigration   when a person comes to a new country to live there permanently

journalist   somone who writes reports for a newspaper

literary agent   person who looks after the business side of an author's work

manuscript   text written by the author in its basic form before being turned into a book

Morse code   system of dots and dashes that represent letters and numbers, transmitted over radio waves to send messages

narrator   person who tells a story

non-fiction   books containing facts and information, rather than made-up stories

proof   pages produced during the preparation of a book for publication

prose   writing that is not poetry

refugee   person who has been forced to leave their home, for example by war or natural disaster

science fiction   story based on science and technology but with made-up elements, often set in a different time or place

seamstress   woman whose job is to sew things

semi-detached   house that is joined to another house on one side

shortlist   final list of candidates for an award, from which the winner is selected

suspenseful   involving much suspense

terrace   row of houses joined together side-by-side

upholstery   material covering for furniture

Victorian   something that dates back to the reign of the British Queen Victoria, 1837–1901

writer's block   problem some writers have when they are unable to think of what to write

INDEX

adapting stories 20, 21
anthologies 4, 37
Ashford 8

Barrett, Anne 9
Belgium 42

Canterbury College
   of Art 12
Carnegie Medal 16,
   19, 36
*Carrot Tops and
   Cottontails* 20
cats 25
Chapman, D.H. 9
characters 21, 22
creative writing
   courses 24
critical reviews 38–39,
   40–41

dialogue 11
drafts 27

*The Eclipse of the
   Century* 34–35, 36
The Ennead 16, 30–31
*Enough is Too Much
   Already* 39

films 25
Fine, Anne 15
Fortean Times 23

Geras, Adèle 39, 41

Handles 19, 32–33
Heathrow Nights 40
The Hillingdon Fox 39
history 10, 23
Hughes, Shirley 9

illustrations, illustrators
   9, 12, 13, 20
inspiration 22, 23

Kersh, Gerald 16
Kipling, Rudyard 16

literary agent 16

Mark, Jan
   art school 12
   awards 16, 19, 36, 37
   childhood and
      schooldays 6–12
   death 25, 43
   family 6, 7, 8, 9
   favourite things 5
   hopes, dreams, and
      ambitions 43
   love of reading 9
   marriage and children
      14
   teaching 13–14, 19, 24
   timeline 44–45
   writer in residence
      (Oxford Polytechnic)
      18–19, 20
   writing method 24,
      26–27
Mark, Neil 14
Masefield, Judith 9
Maupassant, Guy 16
Mitchell, Mary 10
Morse code 22

non-fiction 20, 38
Norfolk 14, 18
North Finchley 7

open endings 27
Oxford 20, 21
Oxford Polytechnic
   18–19, 20

Peet, Mal 38
plays 10, 13, 20
poetry 37
Pullman, Philip 41
Pygmalion 11

radio programmes 20
readers' comments 43
revisions 24, 27
Riding Tycho 22, 27
Ross, Tony 20

Saki (H.H. Munro) 16
science 10, 23
sculpture 12, 31
Shakespeare, William
   10, 13, 40
Shaw, George Bernard
   11
short stories 16, 17
Something in the Air 22

television programmes
   20, 21, 37
*They Do Things
   Differently There* 39
Thunder and Lightnings
   15, 16, 28–29, 36
Trouble Half-Way 37

Useful Idiots 23

Voyager 43

Watts, Bernadette 12, 13
Winterbottom, Michael
   37
World War II 6
writer's block 26
writing tips 19

Titles in the *Writers Uncovered* series include:

HB   0 431 90626 2

HB   0 431 90627 0

HB   0 431 90628 9

HB   0 431 90629 7

HB   0 431 90630 0

HB   0 431 90631 9

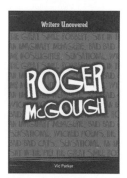

HB   0 431 90632 7

HB   0 431 90633 5

Find out about other titles from Heinemann Library on our website www.heinemann.co.uk/library

Also available from Heinemann Literature:

Hardback   0 435 13062 5

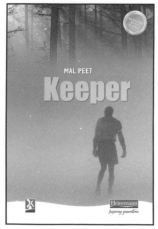

Hardback   0 435 12010 7

Find out about other titles from Heinemann Literature on our website www.heinemann.co.uk/literature